The 12 Talents:
The Must-Have Habits and Attitudes of Effective 21st Century Leaders

The 12
TALENTS

The Must Have Habits and Attitudes of Effective 21st Century Leaders

JOHN E. MICHEL • ANGELA MAIERS • MATTHEW T. FRITZ
GEORGE H. FRITZ • CATIE HARGROVE • JAY S. LEVIN
JEAN MICHEL • HOLLY MICHEL • CATHERINE MICHEL
GARTH SANGINITI • DOUGLAS VANWIGGEREN

The 12 Talents:
The Must Have Habits and Attitudes of Effective 21st Century Leaders

Contributing Teammates

John E. Michel
Angela Maiers
Matthew T. Fritz
George H. Fritz
Catie Hargrove
Jay S. Levin
Jean Michel
Holly Michel
Catherine Michel
Garth Sanginiti
Douglas VanWiggeren

2014

First Printing: 2014

12 Talents Publishing
www.the12talents.com

Dedication

To leaders everywhere who aspire to inspire through their actions and interactions, thank you! Without your engagement and desire to grow, we would have never have been written this book.

To our teams who continue to drive us to new heights, thank you! Without your constant demand for higher performance and better accountability, we would not have had the spark write down these words.

To our partners and clients, current and future, who look to us for guidance, insight and inspiration, thank you! Without your thirst for a better way to explore new possibilities, we couldn't have made a book like this available.

Finally, to our families and friends, who constantly provide us energy and inspiration, thank you! It is your consistent support and encouragement that drove us to share our thoughts in print.

THE 12 TALENTS

THE MUST HAVE HABITS AND ATTITUDES OF EFFECTIVE 21ST CENTURY LEADERS

JOHN E. MICHEL | ANGELA MAIERS | MATTHEW T. FRITZ
GEORGE H. FRITZ | CATIE HARGROVE | JAY S. LEVIN
JEAN MICHEL | HOLLY MICHEL | CATHERINE MICHEL
GARTH SANGINITI | DOUGLAS VANWIGGEREN

Contents

Acknowledgements

We would like to thank the many great leadership thinkers who make writing about this topic fun, easy and inspiring. In particular, we would like to thank the following fundamental thinkers for their work in illuminating the paths that make leadership worth pursuing:

- John Maxwell
- Mike Myatt
- Ken Blanchard
- Anthony Robins
- Jim Collins
- Warren Bennis
- Margaret Wheatley
- Dale Carnegie
- Rosabeth Moss Kantar
- Tony Hsieh
- Peter Drucker
- Daniel H. Pink
- Michael Hyatt

Introduction

By Teammates: John E. Michel & Angela Maiers

A true leader has the confidence to stand alone, the courage to make tough decisions, and the compassion to listen to the needs of others. He does not set out to be a leader, but becomes one by the quality of his actions and the integrity of his intent."

General Douglas MacArthur

The conversation around "must-have" 21st century leadership skills has been in full swing for years. From business to education, classroom to community, the debate on what is a "new skill" or an "always skill" can be both controversial and confusing.

Although it's almost certain we will never all agree on a singular list of skills, strategies, and competencies leaders must embody for success now and in the future, we do know what effectively operating and leading in a dynamic and ever changing 21st Century world requires:

- The ability to see the challenge and the solution, from every angle
- The ability know what questions to ask and when to ask them
- The ability to communicate one's vision passionately and persuasively
- The ability to connect with others and create an enduring relationship
- The ability to understand our strengths and the discipline to improve our weaknesses
- The ability to dream, set audacious goals, and believe they can be accomplished
- The ability to stand out, stand up, and stand beside and knowing when each is required
- The ability to lead, serve and honor others.

12 Talents

Be it liberating the innate genius of teachers and students in the classroom or leading tens of thousands of people to achieve astounding positive effect on the battlefield and boardroom, history and experience confirm that individuals and organizations with these particular attributes are much better equipped to solve any problem, capitalize on every opportunity and create a cycle of positive change that renders no challenge insurmountable.

These abilities, however, are not developed to their full potential naturally. They reflect a willful combination of habits, daily disciplined decisions that successful individuals choose to make, but they also demand a particular attitude and way of thinking about the world and one's place in it. Together, these disciplined habits and critical mindsets, or Habits and Attitudes, provide a comprehensive model for excellence.

1. **Imagination**: The ability to create unique images or ideas. Imagination enables us to leverage our creativity to unlock new, vast and fascinating opportunities.
2. **Self-Awareness**: Possessing a clear understanding of our strengths, shortcomings, motivations and emotions. Self-awareness allows us to better understand other people and positions ourselves to transform informed insight into intentional action.
3. **Courage**: The willingness and ability to face fear, ridicule or rejection in order to stand up for our values and beliefs. Courage reflects a commitment to lean in when it would be easier, safer or more comfortable to fall back.
4. **Adaptability**: The ability to change (or be changed) to fit new circumstances. Adaptability infuses us with the necessary tolerance to accept different circumstances and unexpected conditions without losing momentum.
5. **Perseverance**: The commitment to persist or remain constant when pursuing an idea, purpose or task despite facing obstacles or objections. Perseverance enables us to finish what we've started, no matter how daunting or discouraging the circumstances.

6. **Passion**: Powerful emotions that propel us beyond our current comfort zone in the direction of our potential. Passion is the fuel that transforms bold ideas into tangible realities. It is channeled enthusiasm and excitement in pursuit of bold goals, big dreams, and ambitious agendas.

7. **Curiosity**: A desire to inquire and experience something new, novel or unfamiliar. Curiosity stimulates the mind and frees our creative emotions, opening the door to the most exciting aspects of living.

8. **Empathy**: The ability to selflessly tune in to another person's circumstances, point of view, thoughts and feelings. Empathy reflects our internal capacity to suspend judgment so we connect to others in a way that makes them feel acknowledged and valued.

9. **Resilience**: The capacity to effectively deal with stress, adversity and hardship. Resilience reveals our ability to bend and not break when life throws us unexpected curve balls or thrusts us into unpleasant circumstances.

10. **Compassion**: The ability to identify with and respond to another person in their moment of distress, heartbreak and hurt. Compassion is an altruistic form of selflessness that motivates us to move from passive bystander to active participant in the process of helping to relieve suffering in our surroundings.

11. **Grace**: The willingness to actively extend unmerited favor, kindness or forgiveness to those around us. Grace is a soul-thrilling concept, which equips us to do unto others as we desire others do unto us.

12. **Discipline**: The purposeful application of willpower to accomplishing a given task or effort. The cornerstone of success of every great leader and organization boils down to applying disciplined thought to intentional, well-coordinated action.

Routinely putting into practice the immensely powerful combination of these refined habits and focused attitudes establishes conditions for everyone, both leader and led, to elevate performance, enhance buy-in, and maximize satisfaction. In turn, it fuels the creation of a virtuous cycle of positive change that transforms routine moments into opportunities to achieve results previously thought unimaginable.

Said another way, these 21st Century Habits and Attitudes are much more than a nice list of things TO DO. Rather, they reveal the explicit profile of the learner, worker, and citizen leader the world is expecting each of us TO BE. Therefore, whether we are leading soldiers in a war zone, helping students pass algebra in a classroom or seeking to create a renewed spirit of innovation and excellence within our organization, these Habits and Attitudes will dramatically improve the chances of leadership success in both big and small ventures.

The cornerstone of success for every great leader and organization boils down to applying disciplined thought to intentional, well-coordinated action.

In his brilliant book, *Five Minds for the Future*, Howard Gardner offers a definition of leadership that validates the immense value of these invaluable, must-have 21st century skills. He writes, "A leader is someone who is able, through persuasion and personal example, to change the thoughts, feelings, and behaviors of those whom he seeks to lead." In other words, he highlights how successfully leading people in a dynamic, ever changing world requires us to create the conditions for shared commitment, clear understanding and mutual trust.

Only then, when we succeed in making people feel as though they matter and their efforts are valued—and valuable—will they choose to show up in a way that makes excellence a possibility. Only then will we demonstrate we are leaders worth following.

Chapter 1: Imagination

By Teammate: Doug VanWiggeren

"Imagination is more important than knowledge.
For knowledge is limited to all we now know and
understand, while imagination embraces the entire
world, and all there ever will be to
know and understand."

Albert Einstein

Frequently, in today's dynamic and challenging environment, leaders at all levels must answer questions, develop solutions, and plan strategies for which they have no sure answer and little related past experience. This fact validates the important truth behind the old saying that experience is what we get right after we need it. So what tool can every successful leader use to help them rise above uncertainty and doubt in new situations with unfamiliar challenges? In these cases, a great asset is a good imagination.

The dictionary defines imagination as the ability to form a picture in one's mind of something one has not seen or experienced; the ability to think of new things; and, an ability to deal with a problem. Therefore, imagination is the ability to create unique ideas or images in our minds. Imagination enables us to leverage our creativity to unlock new, vast, and fascinating opportunities.

We all have the ability to imagine. I'll prove it – just for fun, take a minute and think what it would be like to win the lottery. What would you do with the money? What would you buy? Where would you go? Even if we have experience winning lotteries, and not many of us do, my guess is that we are thinking of doing something different, something new that our newfound windfall would make possible – that's imagination.

Unfortunately, in our youth most of us developed an imagination focused on the negative. Out of a natural sense of self-preservation we learned to imagine what would happen if we failed to obey parents or break rules at school. In many of us, the natural creative potential of the imagination we were born with has been channeled toward avoiding painful consequences rather than envisioning potential opportunities. Like other abilities, if we don't use our positive-focused imagination, we eventually lose it. The result is not a lack of imagination for solving problems in our workplaces and homes – instead it is often a misuse of our imagination to find new and innovative ways to avoid responsibility or ignore a challenge. We humans have been very imaginative over the years inventing bureaucratic processes that allow leaders to avoid making decisions while giving the illusion of making progress. Meanwhile opportunities take longer to achieve or are completely thwarted and frustrations build.

Imagine where the world would be today if instead of using our imaginations to avoid and delay, we used our imaginations to look for those wonderful opportunities hiding behind the immediate problem. We need to channel our imagination to "see" past what is immediately evident and "look" beyond our own experience to envision potential opportunities.

Just like every other "muscle" in our body, we need to exercise our imagination to achieve positive results. One way to exercise a positive-focused imagination is to force ourselves to imagine the good things that could result from a situation instead of imagining how "safe" we will be if we use our imagination to avoid responsibility. Ironically, we can begin to strengthen our positive imagination by using our comfortable negative imagination to think of all the wonderful benefits we are giving up by not taking action.

In closing, it is important to note we have all been born with a wonderful ability to imagine things we haven't personally experienced yet. However, most of us have been trained since birth to use our valuable imagination to avoid future pain instead of guiding us toward potential opportunities. It takes work and exercise to develop a positive-focused imagination. We need to intentionally and regularly focus our imagination on potential opportunities and the benefits we could be giving up if we decide to "play it safe." Finally, when we have doubts about our ability to forge ahead on a new path toward future opportunities, we need to remember another wise saying, "In every changing situation, there are opportunities waiting for people who are smart enough to see them."

Chapter 2: Self-Awareness

By Teammate: Garth Sanginiti

"He who knows others is wise. He who knows himself is enlightened."

Lao Tzu

In Parker Brothers® famous board game "Monopoly", players jockey for position to buy, rent and sell property in order to become imaginary tycoons and earn the all-important bragging rights among family and friends. The rules require each player start with $1,500 on the corner marked "Go" and success is ultimately determined by the roll of the dice, a sound investment strategy, a player's ability to negotiate, and, (be honest here!) good ol' fashioned cut-throat competition! One of the basic principles of the game is that players collect $200 every time they pass "Go", unless, of course, they are thrown in jail. Pass "Go" too many times without collecting $200 and players quickly find themselves behind the proverbial 8-ball and unable to effectively compete.

So how does Monopoly relate to self-awareness? Simple. Just as a player collects $200 only when they pass "Go" (without being thrown in jail!), today's 21st century leaders cannot pass "Go" without mastering the art of self-awareness. Self-awareness is a foundational skill of emotional intelligence (EQ) and leaders with high self-awareness are able to increase employee engagement, productivity, and collaboration. In their bestseller "Emotional Intelligence 2.0", Drs. Travis Bradberry and Jean Greaves state, "self-awareness is so important for job performance 83 percent of people who are high in self-awareness are top performers." In addition, as leaders move up in position and responsibility, the importance of self-awareness increases. Those with high self-awareness are able to achieve more through, and with, their teams because of their ability to build lasting relationships, both vertically and horizontally, and both within and outside the organization.

Twenty-first century leaders who are committed to practicing the art of self-awareness recognize their emotions and tendencies as they occur. They possess a clear understanding of their strengths, shortcomings, motivations and emotions. Maintaining high self-awareness allows leaders to better understand other people and position themselves to transform informed insight into intentional action. While leaders who are skilled in this area recognize the people, events and activities that push their buttons, they are also keenly aware of the physical and behavioral reactions associated with their response. They take time to write down their emotions so they can fully appreciate what's happening and recognize the physical and behavioral changes that occur when emotions start to get the best of them. In other words, practicing high self-awareness allows today's leaders to achieve positive outcomes by strengthening relationships. And in today's global marketplace, relationships are the secret sauce that separates success from failure.

In their book "Heart, Smarts, Guts, and Luck" (Harvard Business Review Press) authors – Anthony K Tjan, Richard J Harrington and Tsun-Yan recognize self-awareness as the most important leadership quality. Tjan notes, "The best thing leaders can do to improve their effectiveness is to become more aware of what motivates them and their decision-making." Researchers from Stanford University found, "Among Fortune 500 companies, 90% of leaders who failed, did so because they lacked the interpersonal skill that is a critical component of emotional intelligence." At the Center for Creative Leadership, researchers found almost "half of all CEOs fail at their positions within two years." Their findings indicate failure is not because of a lack of technical or cognitive talents, but because of, "a lack of EQ competencies, that is, inadequate interpersonal skills, lack of sensitivity, inability to handle conflict constructively and poor emotional awareness of others."

Self-awareness does not require a person to suppress or ignore their feelings. Quite the opposite! It requires the individual to recognize the source of their emotions and learn how to push through the discomfort of their emotions. In the acclaimed movie Ray, which chronicles the storied life and career of rhythm and blues musician Ray Charles, a clip captures the moment Ray loses his eyesight. In this unforgettable moment, Ray grapples with his new found reality while his mother wrestles with holding back her natural instincts to console him. Keenly aware of her emotions, she pushes through her discomfort, while also watching her son lean into his discomfort as he learns to rely on his senses of touch and hearing. Recognizing the pain, hurt and apprehension any mother would feel, she chooses to make the deliberate choice to encourage Ray by speaking words of affirmation and setting his life on a positive path.

Whether in our personal lives, or in corporate boardrooms, today's leaders stand to learn from this scene. How much more successful could today's leaders be if they were more self-aware of their emotions? What if instead of being the leader who wears their emotions on their sleeve and is oblivious to how this impacts their team, the leader demonstrated high self-awareness by being in tune with their emotions yet was able to remain calm, cool, and collected during the stressful times? Employee engagement, collaboration and empowerment would increase and relationships would grow stronger and deeper.

Indian nationalist leader Mahatma Gandhi once said, "Our greatness lies not so much in being able to remake the world as in being able to remake ourselves." Being able to remake ourselves begins with self-awareness, for only when one is able to recognize where they are, can they truly begin the journey down the path of improvement. And just like in the game of Monopoly where a player cannot collect $200 until they pass "Go", today's 21st century leaders cannot reach their full potential, nor remake themselves, until they are able to master the skill of self-awareness.

Chapter 3: Courage

By Teammate: Matthew T. Fritz

"Success is not final, failure is not fatal; it is the courage to continue that counts."

Winston Churchill

Richard Branson's first business venture was a mail-order company started with funding accumulated by handing out leaflets outside of concerts. A 15-year old Bill Gates ditched school in Seattle to develop a traffic-measurement program called Traf-O-Data, netting $20k for himself and fellow student, Paul Allen. Colonel Jimmy Doolittle led 80-men in sixteen B-25 bombers barely able to take off from the deck of the USS Hornet on a Tokyo raid in 1942, when landing—even return—was tenuous, at best. And a little girl took on a wicked witch and saved all of Oz, despite the efforts of a self-doubting lion. A common thread binding these four stories can be summed up in one word: courage.

Much has been written on the topic of courage as it applies to leadership. The ability to persevere in the face of negative consequences is, after all, foundational to leadership discussions about risk taking, responsibility, bold action and facing challenges. The inverse of courage, "Submission to Fear," leads to avoidance, hiding and pretending the risk is not there. The result of this path is regret: "I wish I would have done something…" or "I could have started something great." As you may have guessed, the difference between ending up in the history books and an unremarkable life is the level of courage you choose to pursue and the amount of fear you choose to overcome.

Personal courage and your ability to face what you fear can be daunting—especially if the personal choice to be courageous is not popular. Your credibility and your brand—in some cases, your honor—are built upon the level of courage you choose to enact. The same is true whether you are on the battlefield trail, the yellow-brick road, or on the path to the C-suite: courage is a choice made under stress. Such choices have never been easy.

In 1948, Richard and Maurice McDonald completely closed a boomingly successful restaurant in San Bernardino, CA. They did so based on educated-intuition that they could serve their customers even better, but only if they shut their doors to revamp their entire operation. After firing the carhops, shuttering the doors and ripping up the kitchen, the two brothers mechanized their food preparation operation. The streamlined the process with the end-goal of producing quality food in record speeds and affordable prices…and they succeeded. Their courageous move reaped amazing success, allowing them to expand—selling 21 franchises and nine outlets across Southern California.

Enter 52-year old Ray Kroc—who had been selling Multimixers to the McDonalds brothers so they could churn out shakes for their increasingly hungry crowd. In 1954, he traveled to San Bernardino to see why the brothers had been ordering so many shake-mixers and had an epiphany. What started out as a conversation with the McDonalds brothers about opening up more restaurants so he, himself, could sell more Multimixers ended up with a signed contract to begin rolling out the franchise nationwide. When he returned to Chicago, Ray leveraged his credit and his credibility to found the Franchise Realty Corporation and opened the first McDonald's restaurant in Des Plaines, IL. The McDonald's Corporation was chartered in 1960, and Ray bought the full-rights from the McDonald brothers for $2.7M. Today, McDonald's is selling hamburgers to over 46 million people a day from over 34,000 stores around the world in 121 countries and is a marketing symbol known by everybody.

Both the McDonald's brothers and Ray Kroc displayed courage, but their results were dramatically different. The level of success experienced by each can be derived from the level of risk each was willing to take, and the boldness of vision each was inspired to follow. In "Courage in Leadership: From the Battlefield to the Boardroom," Peter Voyer outlines the corporate context of the "Four

Pillars of Leadership" as Loyalty, Knowledge, Integrity and Courage. The latter being the lynchpin of effective leadership. In Peter's words, courage is "having the strength of character to persist and hold on to ideas in the face of opposition." The McDonald's brothers displayed visionary courage and followed their informed intuition to make an uncomfortable choice in closing their doors—what was born revolutionized their business. Ray Kroc displayed leadership courage through his obsession with the potential of the brand—what was born revolutionized the restaurant industry.

In "Courage as a Skill," Kathleen Reardon describes business courage as a "special kind of calculated risk taking. People who become good leaders have a greater than average willingness to make bold moves, but they strengthen their chances of success...through careful deliberation and preparation." What Kathleen describes is what few of us recognize: courage doesn't have to be an innate trait of human performance. It is a skill that can be learned through repeated interaction, learning and leaning into our own discomfort. As with any learning, our success is determined by the goals we set, the level of commitment to growth we display, and our willingness to learn from our mistakes and try again.

Each of us has the ability to find within ourselves a motivation and a drive that can compel us to face adversity and grow through an obstacle. While your courageous moment may not be taking a hill on a battlefield or breaking into the hamburger business, you face obstacles daily providing you with the ability to test, learn and re-apply the lessons you require to stretch your courage in new directions. As Susan Tardanico writes in "10 Traits of Courageous Leaders," demonstrating leadership courage can be scary. However, this is exactly the point. "...it's precisely the kind of behavior that fosters trust and sets a crucial example for others to follow at a time when they'd rather hunker down and wait for the storm to pass." The example you set, for yourself, your team, your family and your community may be exactly what it takes to conquer the next fear, hamburger or wicked witch that stands in your way.

Your yellow-brick road is waiting!

12 Talents

Chapter 4: Adaptability

By Teammate: George H. Fritz

Intelligence is the ability to adapt to change.

Stephen Hawking

Each day brings the possibilities of fresh change and new challenges for everyone.

New technology, new opportunities...new problems. At home and on the job. Whether you work for a paycheck or are running a business. As an entrepreneur, adapting to new challenges and realties occurring in product development, marketing and roll out plans, or real world customer acceptance often falls on you as the driving force behind the business. Yesterday's plans need to be updated, rethought or built upon. Entrepreneurs and leaders at every level have to be ready to tackle change and guide their wards through challenges and uncharted waters--new solutions--and new rewards.

How you react to these challenges speaks much about you and your potential for success.

Are your adaptable?

Do you look at daily challenges as a chance to grow and expand, or as a challenge to yesterday's plans?

Adaptability is one of the most important traits in successful leaders and entrepreneurs.

Adaptability can be defined as the ability to change (or be changed) to fit new circumstances – to see the challenge and the solution from every angle. Adaptability infuses you with the ability to accept different circumstances and unexpected conditions without losing momentum. Adaptability has been called one of "the must have habits and attitudes of effective business leaders!"

Being an adaptable entrepreneur means having a mindset of flexibility. But that's not all – there's a more expanding element in the package deal of an adaptive mindset. With an adaptive mindset, you recognize that when something goes awry, it is not a problem, but an opportunity. These deviations from the plan are opportunities to be creative, change direction – a little or a lot – and make things even better than originally envisioned. You will reach a point where you expect to have such opportunities. This isn't negative thinking. Instead, it is a mindset of looking for ways to improve upon a situation. When something isn't working quite right, that is a signal there's a better way.

How do you react to new challenges?

Do the following traits define you? You live in the moment. You don't see the future as a fixed destination. Instead, you see it as a place you create out of the choices you make right now. You discover your future one choice at a time. This doesn't mean that you don't have plans. You probably do. However, constant adaptability enables you to respond willingly to the demands of the moment even if they pull you away from your plans. Unlike some, you don't resent sudden requests or unforeseen detours. You expect them. They are inevitable. Indeed, on some level you actually look forward to them. You are, at heart, a very flexible person who can stay productive when the demands of work are pulling you in many different directions at once.

If this sounds like you, then you have one of the foundational skills to be an effective entrepreneur.

Entrepreneurs are often advised to stay strong and have an unwavering commitment to an idea; however, this is not always the best plan. Building a company from the ground up is about testing every assumption and reacting as new information emerges. We learn something every day about the industry, our customers and partners, the investors, our team, and ourselves. Being open to where we are wrong and adjusting our approach is the key to the right product, sales, and market strategy. This applies to the small details as well as to big strategy and product decisions. Find the truth rather than sticking to your guns. Be adaptable. Be passionate about building the right product or solving a problem, not about your original idea or solution.

Being adaptable is advantageous at every level. Entrepreneurs in startups and small companies have big advantages over larger companies in the area of adaptability. Shifting strategy for a big company is difficult and you will need to embrace the advantage and quickly make the turns needed to find the right opportunity.

Everyone benefits from being adaptable. Whether people are trying to stay relevant at age 60 in a large corporation, coping with a new job with unfamiliar rules and methods, facing a scary reality that their industry is in danger of becoming extinct, struggling to get donations for their nonprofit in a troubled economy, or – as a result of our current economic crisis – suddenly unemployed and looking for, or starting, a new career path. People of all ages and walks of life are scrambling to deal with the vast changes that are happening in every industry, every profession, and in every part of the world.

As an entrepreneur, you are open to all of these challenges every morning.

To be successful, you're not only expected to keep up, but also find new and creative solutions. While successful entrepreneurs are committed to their vision, they are also willing to adapt their methods or product. As the market changes and new findings are made, entrepreneurs are constantly re-evaluating their efforts and willing to adjust their execution to better serve customers. You may not like having to develop a new product or service, or ditch an existing one, but if that's the way your market is going, can you afford to be left behind? Change happens often and quickly for entrepreneurs, especially during the planning stages as new opportunities and ideas arise. Lack of adaptability can result in unhappy customers, lost profits – and many sleepless nights.

Adaptability does not mean abandoning your plans. It only requires that you review and adjust.

Adaptability is the key to sustainability.

When problems crop up – and they will – always be ready to adapt to new solutions. If you believe problems are an opportunity to adapt and improve, your world will be filled with outcomes better than you ever imagined.

12 Talents

Chapter 5: Perseverance

By Teammate: Holly Michel

"The difference between a successful person and others is not a lack of strength, not a lack of knowledge, but rather a lack in will."

Vince Lombardi Jr.

Before World War Two, Corrie ten Boom was just an ordinary woman living in Amsterdam with her father and sister, working in the family watch making business. However, when Adolf Hitler came to power in the 1930s, it quickly became evident to the ten Boom family that they couldn't simply stand by and watch the senseless Nazi persecution of Jewish citizens. Their response was to open their home to Jewish refugees. No person was turned away from the ten Boom family home.

However, on February 28, 1944, the Nazis received a tip from a Dutch spy that something wasn't quite right with the ten Boom household. After raiding the home, the entire family was arrested, sent to prison, and later sent on to various concentration camps. Corrie and her sister Betsie were sent to Ravensbrück concentration camp after the death of their father, where both women endured unimaginable hardship and struggle. In December of that year, Corrie's beloved sister Betsie died, leaving Corrie the only surviving member of her family.

On New Year's Eve 1944, Corrie was released from the camp. In the years that followed, she travelled across the globe sharing her message of hope and healing with millions of people. Her story of service, faith and incredible perseverance was captured in the bestselling book, the Hiding Place, and continues to inspire people today.

12 Talents

Everyone at some point will face great obstacles in life, using perseverance as a means to succeed. Whether it be: a) a difficult boss to appease throughout the day, knowing that doing a great job is never quite good enough; b) being a single mom, balancing a job and children while praying that she has enough money just to make ends meet; c) growing up in a grim environment or climate hoping that someone is generous enough to provide their next meal; d) or battling just to survive each day in a pain-filled body due to some kind of chronic illness.

So what is perseverance? Is perseverance a mindset? An inherited trait? Alternatively, is it something that can be learned? I would have to say that it's a combination of all three. The definition of perseverance is the commitment to persist or remain constant when pursuing an idea, purpose or task despite facing obstacles or objectives. Perseverance enables us to finish what we've started, no matter how daunting or discouraging the circumstances

I believe what makes perseverance one of the most unique traits is that it enables you to actively choose to respond with a positive attitude no matter what obstacles stand in your way. I have seen individuals use this trait to see the obstacles, not as roadblocks, but challenges in making the correct course adjustments to continue to persevere in hard times and in suffering. They choose to put on their boxing gloves and stay in the fight, using determination to say, "I will never give up and never give in, until the day I die."

I know for me personally, I walk in perseverance each and every day to face an ongoing illness that I have suffered with for the past 16 years. Pain greets me the moment I open my eyes each morning. The severity can change from day to day, hour to hour, minute to minute, but fighting with this disease will never change. Therefore, when I have to surrender the day to my physical pain, I actively choose to have the mindset to never give up in continuing to face it "head on" and make the most out of each and every moment. Trust me; I didn't always grab hold of perseverance to allow me to maneuver through life. I once routinely drowned in a sea of self-pity, hopelessness and despair, letting each wave of adversity drag me deeper into a pit of darkness. And when you fall that far down, the only view you are left with is looking up and watching the world pass you by. However, what I discovered there, which author Shelia Walsh stated perfectly in her book; "God Loves Broken People," is that God lives near the floor. It was there that I found strength, courage and hope. I was shown how to put one foot in the front of the other and actively step into perseverance and continue to use determination to thrive.

So I will leave you with one last thought: Life is not always easy. We may never face living in concentration camps like Corrie ten Boom, but we will all go through turbulent seasons. It's just a part of living. However, when adversity strikes, how are you going to respond? Are you going to let the trial determine your outcome? On the other hand, are you going to respond with perseverance and say, "It's never the trial that makes me stronger, it's what I choose to do with that trial."

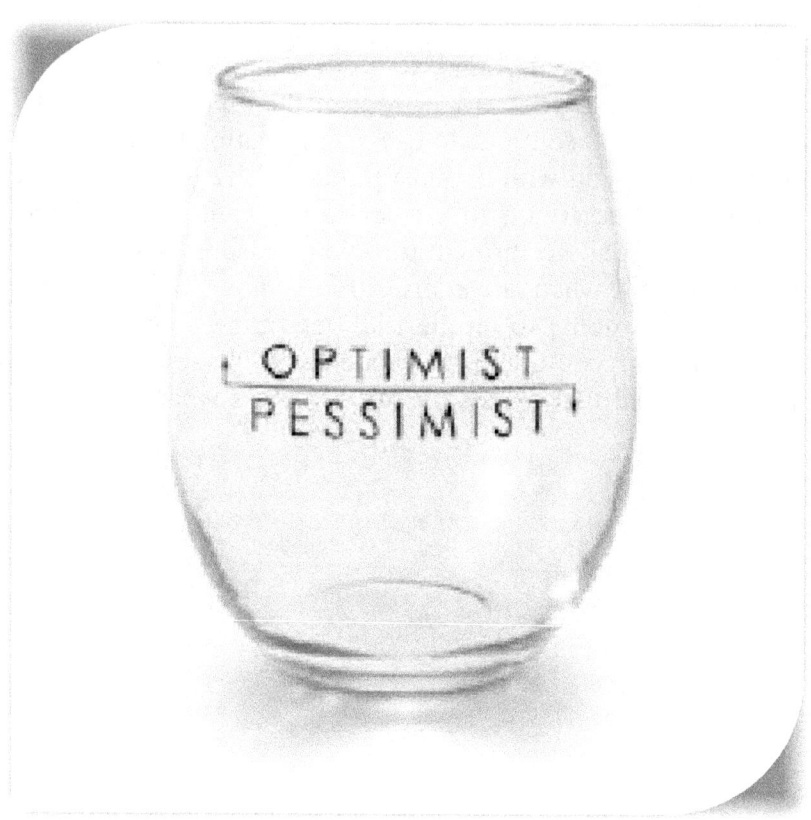

Chapter 6: Passion

By Teammate: Catie Hargrove

*A great leader's courage to fulfill his vision comes
from passion, not position.*

John Maxwell

There are dozens of characteristics that all great leaders must possess such as courage, discipline, empathy, steadfastness, and the list continues. Passion, however, is arguably the quintessential trait of all successful leaders. Passionate leaders, not because of their words or public speaking abilities, innately inspire us. We are drawn to those with overwhelming positive energy and a seemingly unquenchable fire for achieving a goal, reaching a new benchmark or uplifting a group of people to move collectively in a positive direction.

Research on intrinsic motivation and employee engagement tells us that what drives a person to be engaged in their work and to follow a leader is when that leader makes them feel connected to the mission or purpose of the organization. Leaders create that connection for their followers by pairing their passion with their vision, or the ideal future state for the organization. Thus, it should be the goal of every leader to identify their passion and to consistently personify that passion through their leadership.

In Kevin Cashman's book, "Leadership from the Inside," he talks about the three attributes of the most effective leaders possess:

1. *Authenticity*: Well-developed self-awareness that openly faces strengths, vulnerabilities, and development changes.
2. *Influence*: Meaningful communication that resonates with people by reminding them what is genuinely important.
3. *Value Creation*: Passion paired with the aspiration to serve multiple constituencies—self, team, organization,

world, family, community—to sustain performance and contribution over the long term.

All three of these attributes are essential for people to not only understand your passion, but to feel equally compelled to support or to follow your direction.

What is Your Passion?

For some leaders, the hard thing about the concept of leading with passion is simply figuring out what they are passionate about. How does one even know what their passion is, let alone how to influence and lead others via their passion? First and foremost, your passion is the thing that gets you out of bed in the morning. For a police officer, catching "the bad guys" and putting people in jail might not be their passion, but helping protect citizens in their community might be what drives them to be great at what they do. A CEO of a manufacturing company might not be passionate about the product the factory produces, but maybe is passionate about employee safety or providing employment opportunities that pay a living wage in his or her community.

So how does a leader either find their passion, or ensure that what they think is their passion is truly a passion and not just an interest? First and foremost, you must attack this question with unabashed curiosity about what the answers might tell you. If you're leading people, they will want to know what you're passionate about. Therefore, all leaders must occasionally do a short self-assessment to make sure their passion is at the forefront of their leadership strategy.

Here is a quick, ten-question self-assessment to help uncover your passion:

1. What do you fundamentally believe in?
2. What gives you the most energy?
3. What do you believe is your fundamental purpose on earth?
4. What would you do if you could not fail?
5. What is the "thing" you are known for?
6. What comes naturally to you, without effort?

7. What is your best skill or talent that you use to help people?
8. If you could have any job, lead any team or start any business or organization, what would it be, and why?
9. If you could make a difference in the world, what would you be doing?
10. As a leader, what do you want to be remembered for?

Once you've answered these questions, the next step is to determine where you can spend some additional time going deeper into the subject area or field of your passion. The idea is that if you're passionate about something, like customer service, you'll want to spend time researching the companies and organizations who provide the most exceptional customer service (e.g. Zappos or Ritz Carlton). Go a step further and find out how to network with those companies or leaders within those organizations. Even if you're not selling clothes or running a hotel, you can learn a lot of crucial information even by spending time with leaders and organizations that, on the surface, appear to be quite disparate.

Finally, once you've nailed down your passion (or passions, if you're so inclined), you need to figure out how to lead with your passion in mind. How will people know about your passion? How do you demonstrate your passion to those you lead? Quite simply: figure out how to walk the walk and talk the talk.

I work with a senior military leader who is 100% passionate about both the topic and the practice of servant leadership. As a leader, he ensures that he tells his new direct reports about this passion so that they are not surprised when it comes up in conversation. In addition, he commits to writing and speaking about the topic on a regular basis, to share what he knows and what he continually learns about the practice of being a servant leader. Finally, this soldier is committed to putting into practice the elements of servant leadership (empathy, awareness, commitment to the growth of others, etc.) in how he works with individuals, teams and the organization that he leads. Passionate leaders connect with those they lead because they are genuine in their pursuit of fulfilling that passion.

Leading with passion, paired with the aspiration to sustain performance and contribution over time might just be the ultimate goal for any leader. Knowing what drives you to action, to be at your best and then living and leading as if it was your one true calling – that is passionate leadership. From here, your mission is simple: find or rediscover your passion and then go and lead others with that passion in mind each day.

Chapter 7: Curiosity

By Teammate: Matthew T. Fritz

"The important thing is not to stop questioning.
Curiosity has its own reason for existing."

Albert Einstein

A tiny rust-colored dot in the sky has captured the attention of our earthbound minds for as long as humans have gazed into the night sky. In 1609, Galileo Galilei peered through the glass of his new telescope and observed Mars in the heavens. The telescope, itself, had only been patented a year earlier by Dutch eyeglass maker Hans Lippershey. In 365 BCE, Aristotle observed that Mars was further away than the moon, and fortified the Greek sequencing of planets. Almost a thousand years earlier, Egyptians named the visible red-spot they saw moving backwards on the horizon, "Horus." Binding everyone around this heavenly body was a natural human emotion—a foundational trait for genius—curiosity! This basic habit and attitude fueled emotion, research and innovation around this single planet for entire civilizations throughout history. Fast forward to today: who among our ancestors would have thought that looking through a high-powered modern telescope they would see evidence of human-induced change in the Martian environment near what is now called, Gale Crater. The tracks in the dust there were brought about via our topic's namesake, which landed there in 2012—the Mars Science Laboratory appropriately named "Curiosity."

Defining Curiosity

Curiosity is our desire to inquire and experience something new, novel or unfamiliar. Curiosity stimulates the mind and frees your creative emotions, opening the door to the most exciting acts of living. Through curiosity, we enjoy the sight of children learning, businesses breaking into new territories and cats' bounding into paper bags…it is the spark that kindles imagination and ignites passion.

Of course, curiosity does not come without a good deal of peril. One has to wonder what was going through the mind of Christopher Columbus as he sat alone on the deck staring into the great void of the sea in front of him…could he really fall off the edge of the flat world? Did Chuck Yeager ever doubt, if only for a moment, that the aluminum of Glamorous Glennis would truly hold up and continue flying past the as-yet-unbroken sound barrier? Alternatively, a bit closer to home...what happens if I press that big red button with no label on it? This is exactly what makes curiosity so powerful—the unknown! It's the drive to know the unknown that propels us forward, even when there is risk involved.

Clinically, curiosity makes the case for keeping us healthy, making us smarter and helping us stay happy. In 1996, Psychology and Aging published a study involving over 1,000 adults over the age of 60. Those who researchers rated as "curious" were more likely to be alive at the end of the 5-year study. Children who showed traits of high curiosity as early as 3-years old tended to score 12-points higher in IQ by the time they were 11. In their book, "Character Strengths and Virtues," Drs. Chris Peterson and Martin Seligman point out our feeling of happiness and fulfillment in life is satisfied through our own curiosity. With so much to live for and so much to explore, how do we set the conditions for curiosity to thrive in our organization?

Nurturing Curiosity

Leaders have a responsibility to nurture and cultivate curiosity in themselves and in their team that goes beyond the bottom-line. The strategic planning process relies upon your ability to define the gap between the "as is" and the "to be" so you can take your team to new heights. Successful strategies depend upon many minds thinking outside the box—and the leader sets the launch conditions that make this journey possible.

- *Seek:* Crack a book, learn a new skill, solve a mystery (or at least read about one). Consider it aerobics for your brain, or an adventure for your team. Leaning into our own discomfort stretches our notion of what is possible. Doing so as a team in a shared-behavior allows each member to take advantage of the safety net provided by one another. Follow-through on the experience by sharing outcomes, solutions and techniques as a team...thereby building a few new neural pathways for each other along the way. Now you have a common launch platform to share with each other in your collective journey.

- *Stimulate:* Positive Psychologist, Mihaly Cskikszentmihalyi, points out in his TED talk that nothing is interesting to us unless we focus our attention on it. As such, focus on a person, place, thing or activity and allow yourself to notice something new. Study, or attention, illuminates the cracks and fissures that exist between what you know about the subject and what you don't. Sketch a picture of where you want your team to be, and then take a detailed picture of where you are. Study the gap, analyze the differences, and then paint a picture with your team of the destination you envision together. This process fuels the rocket and initiates the countdown.

- *Surprise:* Houston...we have a problem! As the leader, I encourage you to expect the unexpected...then do it! We all have activities in our work and personal lives we have done so often and so repetitively that they have become rote, muscle-memory sequences. Break up the sequence and search for a novel way to complete the same task. When the going gets tough...phone a friend! Surprise yourself with the helping hand of a colleague, supplier or customer who may have a unique solution to the question at hand.

Reach For The Stars!

Blast-off! Any fan of Star Trek can recite from memory the mission of the starship Enterprise: *"to explore strange new worlds, to seek out new life and new civilizations, to boldly go where no man has gone before."* What they might not know is the origin of the last phrase. In 1958, the White House published Introduction to Outer Space in order to pump up enthusiasm for a fledgling space program after Sputnik went into orbit in 1957. This quote from page one summed up our passion and provided the inception moment for many to dedicate themselves to the race that was to come:

12 Talents

"The first of these factors is the compelling urge of man to explore and to discover, the thrust of curiosity that leads men to go where no one has gone before"

Why should your team undertake similar tasks to explore new challenges and go where no organization has gone before? If you've done your research, strategized your course, and built the resilience to handle the journey, the answer is simple...why not?

Chapter 8: Empathy

By Teammate: John E. Michel

"The last of the human freedoms is to choose one's attitudes."

Victor Frankl

Viktor Frankl was an incredible person by many measures. He was a brilliant academic, a survivor of three years in four different concentration camps during the Holocaust, a pioneering neurologist/psychiatrist in Vienna following World War II, and an inspirational author. Most notable, however, is that his finest moments came when leadership was thrust upon him in the bleakest of times.

Despite enduring the atrocities of four Nazi concentration camps, the most infamous being Auschwitz, and losing his wife and parents to them, Frankl managed to find what few others could during such a dark period in our world's history: a meaningful purpose for living. Instead of allowing the despairing conditions he found himself in to overwhelm or engulf him, Frankl choose to transform his present circumstances into an opportunity to grow in ways he didn't think possible. How? By resisting the tendency to turn inward and refusing to focus only on his challenges by willfully orienting outward and discovering what he could do to help lighten the load, life the spirits and selflessly serve those around him.

After the war, Frankl told about his varied trials, tribulations, and professional experiences in a series of books that continue to be counted among the most influential of our time. In fact, his writings are largely regarded as masterpieces for their ability to paint images of seemingly average individuals, whose empathy for the plight of others, challenges each of us to re-think our notions of what constitutes an extraordinary person or a truly successful leader.

If you are interested in improving your ability to lead yourself and others more effectively, let me share three vital lessons from Frankl's life experience that can help you.

Finding Meaning through Service

Perhaps the most significant aspect of Frankl's personal transformation from successful professional and beloved family man, to purposeful leader, occurred as a result of what he saw transpiring in the daily events of the Nazi death camps. Events which, over time, taught him firsthand how one of the most important things a leader can do for those in their care is to learn to see events through another's eyes or walk a mile in their shoes.

In his inspirational memoir, "Man's Search for Meaning," Frankl recounts how over time he became transfixed at the sight of others willfully setting aside their own hardships in order to reach out in service to those who needed their help the most. In one account, he recalls a particularly cold morning when he and other prisoners were forced to stumble in the darkness, over big stones and through large puddles, along the one road leading from the camp. The guards were shouting at the prisoners, driving them forward with the butts of their rifles. The only way some of these prisoners were able to make it was by supporting themselves on their neighbor's arm. Hardly a word was spoken; the icy wind did not encourage talk. However, the prisoners' concern for one another was readily expressed in their selfless actions and provided the physical and emotional strength necessary to overcome the cruelty they collectively faced.

Little by little, in the midst of one of our world's darkest moments, Frankl discovered the transformative ability of selflessness to overpower selfishness. It was a discovery that even today serves to remind those of us wanting to become better leaders how developing a great sense of caring for all people, foes as well as friends alike, requires we learn to routinely look beyond ourselves by making empathy an indispensable part of our lives.

Choosing to See Beyond Ourselves

In his international bestseller "The Courageous Follower," Ira Chaleff says that as leaders, "we can model any characteristic we possess or develop, but the most important one to model may be empathy."

In simplest terms, empathy is the ability to put oneself in another's shoes. Alternatively, in the words of psychiatrist Alfred Adler, empathy is "to see with the eyes of another, to hear with the ears of another, and to feel with the heart of another." Unlike sympathy, where you choose to remain an outsider content on viewing the situation from a distance, empathy actively involves the observer. There is an intentional emotional connection made with the other person as you make the choice to better understand what they are seeing, feeling, or experiencing.

Why does the importance of empathy still seem so hard to accept? Is it a practice that is only well suited for our homes or worship spaces but inappropriate for our workplaces?

Sadly, I believe that this remains a common misconception.

Admittedly, empathy seems to have little place in the traditional top-down model of leadership. Perhaps because choosing to see events through another's eyes or walk a mile in their shoes smacks of weakness. It sounds soft and mushy and doesn't resonate well with the vigorous phrases we often associate with leadership.

Words such as vision and daring, conviction and courage, assertiveness and integrity, naturally come to mind. Empathy doesn't often make the leadership cut. Nevertheless, empathy, seeing with the eyes of another, hearing with the ears of another, and feeling with the heart of another, demonstrates our capacity and willingness to project ourselves into the position of another.

Truth is, empathy, being open to understanding the perspectives, emotions, thoughts, concerns, and motives of others is not about embracing blind agreement in order to please those around you. Rather, it's about being open to better understanding others and working to gain an increased appreciation for their circumstances.

Recognizing Everyone Has Value

One of my favorite examples of the importance of learning to appreciate the innate value and worth of every person we encounter comes from a true story from a 1996 edition of Guideposts. To this day, it is a piece I reread periodically to remind me of the importance of practicing empathy in our lives:

> "During my second month of nursing school, our professor gave us a pop quiz. I was a conscientious student and breezed through the questions, until I read the last one: 'What is the first name of the woman who cleans the school?'
>
> Surely, this was some kind of joke. I had seen the cleaning woman several times. She was tall, dark-haired, and in her fifties, but how would I know her name? I handed in my paper, leaving the last question blank.
>
> Before the class ended, one student asked if the last question would count toward the quiz grade. 'Absolutely,' said the professor. 'In your careers you will meet many people. All are significant. They deserve your attention and care.'"

I've never forgotten that lesson. I also learned her name was Dorothy.

As this simple but powerful example affirms, empathy empowers you to build and develop genuine appreciation for those around you; enables you to gain a greater awareness of the needs of those around you; and encourages you to create an environment of open communication and more effective feedback so others feel safe enough to be who they really are. All of which, mind you, are essential if you want to create conditions for trust, transparency, collaboration and mutual appreciation to flourish around you.

Victor Frankl's time in the concentration camps teaches us that no matter how daunting our circumstances, situations or surroundings, when we choose to be generous with others when we don't have to be; show kindness and act with compassion with others when it's not easy; and give freely of ourselves for the benefit of another when doing the minimum is all others expect to see, nothing becomes impossible. Then perhaps you too will discover what Frankl truly meant when he wrote, "we who lived in concentration camps can remember the men who walked through the huts comforting others, giving away their last piece of bread. They may have been few in number, but they offer sufficient proof that everything can be taken from a man but one thing: the last of human freedoms - to choose one's attitude in any given set of circumstances - to choose one's own way."

How are you choosing, today?

Chapter 9: Resilience

By Teammate: Jean Michel

When people talk, listen completely.
Most people never listen.

Ernest Hemingway

Personal resilience and the ability to bounce back from challenging situations are becoming increasingly important in modern day life. Resilient people are able to persist in the face of challenges and to bounce back from adversity. Best of all, ample data confirms resilience is a teachable skill.

People are not born resilient; they become resilient through life experiences or training. Research has shown that when resilient people encounter adverse events they tend to come out on the other side stronger that they were initially. Conversely, less resilient individuals have a tendency to be more negatively impacted by adverse events to the point of, at times, of reverting to self-defeating behaviors as a seemingly suitable coping mechanism.

I have certainly found this to be true in my own life. Born in France at the end of World War II to a family who lost their business to the war, we faced many of the same hardships experienced by my countrymen. We moved frequently and lived very sparsely. However, more than half a century before I knew anything about resilience and positive psychology, I acquired two traits, in particular, that saw me through these hardships and shaped my life; Optimism and Gratitude.

This engrained optimism allowed me to dream big. As a young boy, I lived close to a United States Air Force base in France and came to learn about the United States and its people. It was during this same period that I also came to appreciate all that America selflessly sacrificed to save Europe from the terror and tyranny of Nazi Germany. To me, America represented everything that was right in this world. By the time I was 14 I decided that I would one day become an American and join the U.S. Air Force.

By age 16 I started the laborious immigration visa process (some things never change with time), and secured a job to raise the funds for the boat ticket that would move me toward my seemingly unreachable dream. A year later my visa came through and I had saved enough for a one-way ticket to New York City on the SS United States. All of a sudden, my greatest hopes and dreams became a realistic opportunity. Needless to say, I was grateful that I was able to achieve this milestone so quickly.

Soon I was on my way. I must confess that as the ship's horn blew signaling we had left the harbor and the lights of France slowly faded into the darkness, the sadness of leaving my family and everything that was familiar to me was a little frightening. Yet instead of being overcome by fear of what I was leaving behind, a natural sense of optimism kicked in and reminded me I was securely on my way to realizing my own "impossible dream".

After five days crossing a vast Atlantic Ocean, I was anxious to catch my first glimpse of my newly adopted home. It happened early in the morning on a cold November morning. Climbing to the highest deck, I waited for my first glimpse of America. It was a long wait as I had gone out a little too early. Several hours later, my pulse started to race as I began to make out lights in the distance. The lights of New York City. Soon thereafter, the Statue of Liberty came into full view and I knew then that I had reached the first important milestone of an exciting new life.

With all my worldly possessions packed into a single suitcase, my heart soared knowing that my "impossible dream" was becoming reality. I knew that the next challenge was going to be joining the Air Force but I was convinced that I could do it. Sixty days later, almost to the day, I was on my way to Lackland Air Force Base as a newly minted Airman Basic in the USAF.

More than five decades have passed since that memorable November morning and this year, I complete 52 years of government service to our great country (30 years as an active duty Air Force member and 22 years as a civilian employee). In that time, from the jungle of Vietnam to the hot sands of Southwest Asia and many points in between, I have encountered countless challenging situations which, through the grace of God and the power of resilience, I was able to effectively navigate.

As I wrap this up, let me leave you with three practical ways I have learned you can use to increase your own reservoir of resilience:

Move Out – Thinking about what you want to do or be isn't sufficient to accomplish anything. You have to actually do something to transform your dreams from mere fantasy to reality. Moving out in a well-thought out direction gives you the power to change any situation. Ask yourself: What would you do if you knew you would not fail? What could you achieve? Take it from a lifelong dreamer and optimistic doer – be brave and just do it. Even if it doesn't work out exactly the way you want it to, I promise you that you'll be better for trying.

Be Real – Let me tell you right up front that you are going to fail. Failure is the price of progress. It is also an amazing developer of resilience, as failure requires you to reach down deep inside yourself to find the inner strength to persevere when it is much easier to quit. The key is to commit to not take failure personally. If something doesn't work, don't give yourself a hard time; move on. Look towards the doors that are just about to open for the opportunities they are and see the doors that close as a clear sign it is time to move on.

Serve Others – I learned early in my life the sure path to success isn't found in merely pursing your own agenda but rather, in making it a priority to selflessly serve those around you. Service not only makes you healthier physically, it improves your mood, positively contributes to your community and connects you more deeply to other people. I have been blessed in the last several years with the privilege of developing programs for our USAF Airmen and their families that equip them with the tools they need to face life's adversities and come out stronger on the other side. My hope is that their lives will be enriched and more fulfilling.

As for me, I am looking for the next challenge to take on – after all, there are still new oceans to cross, mountains to climb, frontiers to conquer, and many more stories to write!!!

I urge you to pursue your own "impossible dream." I can promise you that you will not regret it!

12 Talents

Chapter 10: Compassion

By Teammate: Catherine Michel

"Love and Compassion are necessities, not luxuries. Without them, humanity cannot survive."

The Dalai Lama

In 2010, Parade Magazine ran an intriguing article regarding Compassion in America. In the article, Patrick Covington, CEO of the Federal Corporation for National and Community Service noted that historically, during a season of employment hardships, the numbers of volunteers in communities typically went down. However, in the new season of growing unemployment, there appeared to be a "compassion boom" with people actively engaged in volunteer efforts that further connected them to their communities. Covington reported that in addition to honing job skills via volunteer efforts, he believed that part of what was driving the Compassion Boom was a "growing understanding that service is an essential tool to achieve community and national goals".

The numbers from the polls completed by Parade Magazine provide some heartwarming proof that Americans, as a whole, appear to be service-hearted. 94% of those polled believed that it is "important to be personally involved in supporting causes we believe in" on a community level, 91% believed this was important in the world at large. Most notable however, is that 78%, or 3 out of 4 Americans, believe that the actions of one person can indeed improve the world. Those are encouraging statistics indeed.

In addition to polling American attitudes regarding compassion and volunteer efforts, the poll also went on to explain what exactly tips a well-intentioned person to be a person of service...and this is where it gets interesting:

"More than two-thirds (68%) say personal experience has been a major impetus, with 40% saying their motivating experience was a positive one, as in 'someone did something good for me and I want to give back". A family member or a friend's request (33%) and learning about an issue from the news (28%) were other catalysts."

I would have guessed that times of trouble, despair and hardship would have been the prevailing experience that moved or motivated someone to want to help someone else move above and beyond hardship. It's an encouraging note that the opposite is true. That goodness does indeed beget acts of goodness.

So we know, via polling, that most Americans not only want to be generous in service to others, but they actively engage in conscious efforts to "pay it forward." With such a large number of the population being like-minded in these efforts, the obvious question would be "why"?

The question as to why we are wired to spread goodness may be explained by the science of compassion as a behavior. In 2012, at The Science of Compassion: Origins, Measures and Interventions conference in Telluride, Colorado, an impressive panel of intellectuals and researchers came together to explore and elaborate on cutting edge research of the "biological, physical and behavioral properties of compassion". Specifically, the panel elaborated on their findings and determined there were several survival instincts that create the environment for compassion to grow and thrive. In summary, here is what they found:

1. ***Compassion is push-pull****:* The gist of this biological determinant is that the safer one's environment is in terms of trust, support and safety, the stronger ones biological mechanism of nurturing and care giving can be promoted and expanded upon. Simply said, the safer we feel, the more we want to spread that sense of well-being to others. The real kicker in this discovery is that if compassion can be traced to a biological element that is satisfied through lack of self-preservation – by knowing we are safe to help others – than that "trigger" can be trained and practiced.

2. ***Compassion hinges upon mindfulness****:* Here's where they describe the ability to train oneself to be more compassionate. In summary, training yourself to be more compassionate begins with

training yourself to live in the moment…to keep your mind, your perspective and your focus on the situation at hand. By keeping your mind from wandering, judgment, fear and anticipation are kept from creeping into the space where our conscious compassion is attempting to bloom and grow. In essence, a mind that is firmly planted in the present during times of struggle or hardship is better equipped to respond in a truly compassionate manner.

3. ***Brains like helping the group more than helping the self:*** This is the actual brain chemistry involved in acts of compassion-and it's pretty cool stuff. It turns out that the warm feeling you get when you've taken part in something that brings someone comfort, peace or joy is actually a response from the brain's pleasure systems. Dr. Jamil Zaki, professor of Psychology at Stanford explains, "humans are the champions of kindness". His studies reveal that brain imaging data suggest that the brain responds significantly and positively when doing something for the group.

What this recent research confirms is that leaders who exercise compassion produce loyal, dedicated, and passionate employees. In fact, numerous studies have found that workplaces led by compassionate bosses enjoy increased rates of employee satisfaction, greater employee engagement, lower levels of overall stress and fewer reported sick days. In their report, "*What Good is Compassion at Work?*" researcher Jane Dutton and colleagues from the University of Michigan identify a "cascading effect," whereby experiencing compassion at work generates positive emotion and, in turn, shapes employees' long-term attitudes and behaviors.

As a leader, the more you understand what people need and what people's anxieties and worries are, the more effective you will be at working with them. The more compassionate leader you are, the less you are worked up about little stuff and the more you focus on what really needs to be done to bring out the best in everyone—beginning with yourself.

Why not resolve to get started today?

12 Talents

Chapter 11: Grace

By Teammate: John E. Michel

I do not at all understand the mystery of grace – only that it meets us where we are but does not leave us where it found us.

Anne Lamott

A popular Russian tale recounts a time when Nicholas II was the Czar of Russia, a father enlisted his son in the military with the hope of instilling discipline and direction in his life. Among other things, the young man had a weakness for gambling, and the conditions of military life seemed to hurt rather than help.

His army job was bookkeeping. As his gambling debts grew, he borrowed money from the outpost treasury to pay his debts. He kept losing instead of winning and sank deeper and deeper into debt.

One night, contemplating his horrible situation, the young soldier added up his debts. When he saw the immense total, he wrote a cross the ledger, "so great a debt, who can pay?" He decided to take his own life. He sat back in his chair; gun in hand, to reflect for a few minutes. As he contemplated the sad conditions of his life and his impending death, he dozed off.

Czar Nicholas II was inspecting the outpost that night. When he entered the bookkeeper's shack, he saw the sleeping soldier, the loaded gun, and the revealing ledger.

When the soldier awoke, he stared at the ledger in disbelief, reading his words, "so great a debt, who can pay?" Underneath were the words, "Paid in full, Czar Nicholas II!"

Can you imagine how this young man must have felt in that moment? After all, given his countless mistakes and racking up debt he could never possibly repay, here he was with a balanced ledger – a clean slate. Despite doing nothing to warrant such generosity, he was now a free man. His new chance at life was an unwarranted and unexpected gift from the most unlikely of sources.

The Greek's have a term that beautifully captures the essence of this illustration. It is the verb *charis,* from which we derive the term grace. To the Greeks, anything of beauty, favor, or delight in which a person could rejoice was a form of grace. In our contemporary translation, grace enjoys an even deeper, more profound translation, meaning the willful exercise of love, kindness, mercy, favor; or disposition to benefit or serve another. In essence, grace is synonymous with showing unmerited concern or favor to someone. And, as the example of Czar Nicholas II affirms, it's not necessarily because someone deserves it, but simply because we choose to freely grant it.

Admittedly, extending grace is not always easy. In our own lives it means intentionally loving the unlovable, those who seem intent on stretching rules, pushing our buttons, even talking poorly of us and to us. Extending grace also means we choose to respond contrary to our natural inclinations. For instance, instead of responding with a glare, a sharp retort, or with icy silence when someone has frustrated, insulted or wrongly accused us, we choose instead to treat the other person better than they have chosen to treat us.

Does extending grace as a leader really matter, you may wonder? Without a doubt! Authors Bill Thrall, Bruce McNicol and Ken McElrath in their book, "The Ascent of a Leader," share how environments where grace abounds are characterized by higher satisfaction, increased engagement, improved trust, and heightened productivity. They add how leaders who are grace-full help people feel safe to be themselves, to live authentically, celebrate each other, laugh more frequently, and extend grace themselves more liberally. In an organization where grace abounds it's common to find a supportive atmosphere where the seeds of mutually satisfying relationships are frequently and intentionally planted and nurtured and people do not feel constrained by strict adherence to a particular set of do's and don'ts in order to feel accepted, affirmed, or appreciated. Given these profoundly positive effects, what can you do today to begin being more Grace-Full in your own sphere of influence? Start by:

- Intentionally speaking words that build up, not tear down;
- Focusing more on others' needs rather than merely satisfying your own;
- Saying, "I'm sorry", and "I was wrong" without being afraid;
- Not always keeping score of what is fair;
- Not condemning or giving up on people; and,
- Taking every opportunity to emphasize mercy, not justice.

The fact of the matter is, if you want to create a high-performing organization, then you have to be willing to extend grace. I'm not saying you have to dismiss poor performance, overlook situations you know are wrong, or not hold people accountable for failing to achieve established standards. However, I am telling you that unless grace is present, people will not take risks, they won't learn or grow in their own leadership abilities, and they will fear failure so much they won't even get close to achieving their individual potential – making it difficult or even impossible for the organization to reach its potential as well.

So the next time you find it difficult to extend unmerited concern or favor to someone when they fail, fall short of your expectations, or just plain frustrate you to no end, remember the lesson of Czar Nicholas II: Grace is one of the most important gifts a leader can offer their people. Testimony to the reality that grace, the willful exercise of love, kindness, mercy, favor; or disposition to benefit or serve another, is as much a treasure we bestow on others as it is a treasure we share with ourselves.

Whose ledger can you balance today? Whose slate can you wipe clean so they can begin anew?

12 Talents

Chapter 12: Discipline

By Teammate: Jay S. Levin

Self-control is the chief element in self-respect;
and self-respect is the chief element in courage.

Thucydides, The History of the Peloponnesian War

Who we are, in relation to the practice and adherence to discipline, defines us. What we become, as a result of discipline, makes or breaks us. You don't have to search your feelings too deeply to know it's true. At different points in our personal lives and professional careers, we come face to face with discipline...or the lack thereof.

For some, it is imposed upon us from outside influences. For others it's wrought of an internal calling or mandate. For some it is the reason for our accomplishments. For others it's the source of blame, failure, and even anger, because we know we've lacked it. No matter who we are, how accomplished we've become or aspire to be – when we look the rigor of discipline in the eye, what we see in return mirrors us – defining for us in its image a critical image of our character and sense of self-worth.

The image we choose to identify with also defines us. And, as we know all too well, how we see ourselves affects and influences how we see others and boomeranging back to us in return – impacting how those around us – see us.

As a former Monk and Priest in a religious order, few things I've faced have challenged me as much as my relationship with discipline.

Discipline has two facings: internal and external. Internally applied discipline harnesses our thoughts, attitudes and emotions. Externally directed, discipline drives action and habits.

Internally, discipline can be seen as a Roman gladiator; Warrior; Charioteer; each commanding five powerful thoroughbred horses.

All, united and obedient under his direction. All marshaled by his control. Five horses. Five senses. The chariot, our life. Our work. Company. Our leadership.

Command here in this classic old Roman and ancient East Indian metaphor represents the result of our ability to exercise discipline and control over ourselves and the wild horses of our desires, emotions and their reactions.

Externally applied discipline is to effective, scalable leadership what a drive train is to any vehicle of any size. Think, the essential component delivering power to the wheels. Without it, any movement toward a destination is not possible.

General Douglas MacArthur addresses the habit of discipline and its internal and external facings best when he said,

> *"A true leader has the confidence to stand alone, the courage to make tough decisions, and the compassion to listen to the needs of others. He does not set out to be a leader, but becomes one by the quality of his actions and the integrity of his intent."*

Internal and externally focused discipline is the result of an application of directed willpower. We have another name for this phenomenon. It is called memory. Memory of purpose; Of intent; Of passion; Commitment; Of higher calling.

Without memory of purpose discipline is trivialized. When memory of meaning is lost – the self-imposed controls that bring the cultivation and sustainability of discipline about – are marginalized.

As a former Monk, often cloistered in a forest monastery, I came to understand the truth of American Sociologist and founder of Behavioral Sociology and Exchange Theory, George Caspar Homans, when he declared; *"Liberty is a beloved discipline."*

True leadership embodies the discipline, courage and the liberty to stand and remain neutral amidst the swirling temptations of emotional reactions that encircle us - clouding and obscuring our clear judgment and subsequent ability to affect better professional and personal outcomes.

The presence of discipline in leadership signals more the "how" of leading rather than the "what" or "why" of authority. There's a difference to consider.

Think of discipline as a critical Key Performance Indicator (KPI) of effective leadership.

If the habit doesn't appear on your personal dashboard of best practices – add it.

Measure it. Test it. Determine ways to hold yourself accountable for its expression. For example, ask yourself this, when I assess my own degree of discipline how do I know if others assess me in the same way I assess myself. How can we know? Unless, we ask those around us. Even that asking, as I am sure you will agree, takes discipline.

Rely on those your trust at all levels in your organization to offer feedback.

Allow it. Depend on it. Without it, blind spots creep into our leadership practice.

A blind spot, not knowing what we don't know, limits our ability to lead from a clear point of view. It also handicaps our capacity to influence others that report to us as well as those for whom we are responsible.

Without radial feedback we as leaders remain subject matter experts locked in an "I'm-the-expert-who-has-to-tell-you-what-to-do" mode rather than enablers and influencers operating from an ask mode and empowering and promoting the inherent intelligence around us.

Overcoming the ego's temptation to continually tell, to constantly direct and command under all conditions takes practiced discipline. Encouraging and drawing out radial intelligence necessitates discipline.

I know of one self-professed coach who is proud of her discipline to listen. It doesn't dawn on her though that she is directing all the answers her way by the set-up of her questions – which are all designed to get her the answers she wants to hear, so she can tell – not what the client needs, but what she needs. That's not the discipline of surrendering control. It's the masking of it. Her approach isn't listening. That approach is just telling in a different manner.

A student of a great Israeli Rabbi once told me an expression. "If your giving doesn't hurt, you're not giving enough." The same principle can be applied to exercising discipline.

Promoting and drawing out collective intelligence requires on-going cultivation. Doing so means embracing discipline to allow others to take credit rather than continually seeking applause and recognition for ourselves.

Dismantling siloed-thinking and operating and creating cultures of transparency where each clearly understands the solid benefit line their individual contribution makes to the organization, requires continual discipline if we are to truly serve others more selflessly.

The art, practice and continual cultivation of internal and external discipline go hand-in-hand with our capacity for self-regulation.

Self-regulation simply put is our ability to control or redirect dysfunctional impulses and emotions and our capacity to suspend judgment and conclusions so as to think clearly before impulsively responding. The connection between the need for discipline and ability to self-regulate is apparent.

The disciplining practice of self-regulation evidences itself in leaders when:

1. Stress is managed and not allowed to control situations, events or outcomes.
2. Effects of stress are not taken out on others.
3. Negativity is not permitted to interfere in working relationships.
4. Criticism does not affect right outcome.
5. Personal balance equalizes practical and emotional aspects of a situation.
6. Personal poise enables appropriate decisions to occur while managing emotions.
7. Emotional reactions and biases do not affect or distort situational clarity.

If self-regulation and discipline are areas you suspect are needing improvement, here are 15 "do's" to help you mature into a more effective person and seasoned leader;

1. Define specific discipline development goals.
2. Create specific milestone dates for achievement.
3. Clarify why each goal is important to you personally and professionally.
4. Target the specific positive emotion driving each of your goals.
5. Understand specifically what success will look like when your goals are met.
6. Ask yourself what will I get out of being more disciplined?
7. Display your discipline goals were you can see and be reminded of them daily.
8. Determine the best specific upcoming events or situations to put your discipline into practice.
9. Ask trusted people to hold you accountable for reaching your desired goals.
10. Celebrate your accomplishments. Big or small.
11. Assess your feedback, your progress and learn from your mistakes.
12. Find role models who mirror the discipline you want to achieve.
13. Are you relying only on yourself for that evaluation?
14. Alternatively, are you disciplined enough to invite others to assess you as well?
15. Ask yourself how honest and impartial your sources of feedback are.

Inner discipline, order and control of self, brings freedom. Not bondage. The freedom to become and achieve what others cannot imagine is won through effort.

Overcoming bias thinking and expressing true leadership requires inner freedom. "Liberty," as George Caspar Homans stated, "is a beloved discipline."

In the spirit of liberty, I encourage you to embrace discipline. Befriend it. Allow it to assist and support the realization of your potential.

12 Talents

About The 12 Talents

12 Talents, LLC is a revitalization firm that specializes in bringing out the best in people and organizations. Our organization helps improve client profitability, enhance employee engagement and maximize customer satisfaction. In a nutshell, *12 Talents* is the spark igniting the potential of people and organizations to flourish, thrive and become Fully Alive.

Founded in 2013, *12 Talents, LLC* is the creation of John E. Michel and Matthew T. Fritz—both highly decorated former senior military leaders with high records of performance. Having successfully led multiple award-winning organizations in both peacetime and wartime, they and their team bring an unprecedented level of expertise in a host of domains ranging from strategy development, leading complex change, executive coaching, organizational enhancement, emotional intelligence and appreciative inquiry.

Our team of specialized leaders, world-benders and universe-denters is eager to help you tackle your challenges. Please seek us at support@12talents.com to explore how we can work with you to make positive strides for you and your team!